COPING WITH

HOMELESSNESS

Marcia Amidon Lüsted

Published in 2018 by The Rosen Publishing Group, Inc.
29 East 21st Street, New York, NY 10010

First Edition

Library of Congress Cataloging-in-Publication Data

Names: Lüsted, Marcia Amidon, author.
Title: Coping with homelessness / Marcia Amidon Lüsted.
Description: New York : Rosen Publishing, 2018 | Series: Coping | Audience: Grades 7–12. | Includes bibliographical references and index.
Identifiers: LCCN 2017016805 | ISBN 9781508176916 (library bound) | ISBN 9781508178514 (paperback)
Subjects: LCSH: Homelessness—Juvenile literature. | Homeless teenagers—Juvenile literature. | Homeless persons—Services for—Juvenile literature.
Classification: LCC HV4493 .L87 2017 | DDC 362.5/92—dc23
LC record available at https://lccn.loc.gov/2017016805

Manufactured in China

CONTENTS

INTRODUCTION

I t was a cold winter night in a pleasant suburban neighborhood. Families were safely inside their warm homes, protected from the bitter temperatures. It was a common scene in towns all across the United States.

However, in this neighborhood, a young woman named Karen was walking down the street in the freezing night air. She was only fifteen years old, and her mother had just kicked her out of their house. Her mother had mental health issues that made it difficult for Karen to be there. Exhausted and desperately needing to get warm, Karen stayed with a friend for a few days until the family asked her to leave. She told her story to the Covenant House shelter. "I spent the night on a grate," Karen said. After an unsuccessful attempt at living at home, Karen was homeless again a year later. This time, she could not find any friends willing to put her up, even for a few days. "When my friend wouldn't let me stay at her house, I stayed in her backyard, but the family didn't even know it," Karen admitted. It was cold, but at least it was safe.

Going to school and living a normal life was no longer an option. Karen's life became centered around trying to find somewhere warm to stay. She wandered the streets trying to find a safe, warm location. She

A homeless man stands over a steam vent in an attempt to stay warm during an ice-cold Philadelphia winter.

would go to all-night restaurants and order a single cup of coffee, sipping it slowly until she was asked to leave. The best thing she could find was a hot-air grate on the street, where the warm air might keep her from freezing to death. "You worry about freezing to death... you worry about being robbed and beaten up...about where you're going to get something to eat." She stole food from grocery stores. "They saw me, but they didn't chase me because they could tell that I needed it." Karen finally found a place in a homeless shelter for children and teens.

Karen's story is just one of many, many stories about children, teens, adults, and families who are forced to live on the streets. These people may not fit accepted preconceptions: they may have jobs, have come from wealthy households, or be top students in their schools. But for reasons that can include economic circumstances, ill health, or abusive situations, they find that they no longer have permanent homes of their own.

Homelessness is a complicated issue both for those who are affected by it and those who deal with homeless people on a regular basis and try to help them. It is often a terrifying experience to be homeless, but no one who is going through it is ever alone. There is help out there for coping with homelessness and for finding a way out of it.

Who Are Today's Homeless?

CHAPTER ONE

Homeless people are a common sight on city streets, huddled in doorways or in makeshift shelters of cardboard and old blankets. But these homeless people are only one small portion of the larger number of people who have no permanent place to call home.

Who They Are

According to the United States Department of Housing and Urban Development (HUD), on a single night in 2016, 549,928 people were homeless. Of this group, 68 percent were staying in emergency shelters or other forms of transitional housing, while 32 percent were unsheltered, meaning that they were living in unsheltered locations, such

Homeless teens often panhandle for money on the streets; sometimes they will use signs as a way to ask for donations.

as on the street or in abandoned buildings. Of these homeless people, 31 percent were children and teens younger than the age of twenty-four, and 69 percent were adults.

Homelessness includes people of every age, from children to the elderly, and both employed and unemployed people. According to Greendoors statistics on homelessness on a given night:

- 25 percent suffer from mental illness, including schizophrenia, bipolar disorder, and depression.
- 17 percent are considered chronically homeless.
- 13 percent are fleeing domestic violence.
- 12 percent are veterans.

Beyond these groups, the people most at risk for becoming homeless are those living below the poverty level, the working poor (people who can't earn enough to survive), single parent families, people recently released from prison,

Homeless teens in particular may find themselves living "rough," which means that they are sleeping on the streets without shelter.

and teens who have gotten too old for the foster care system. The elderly are also a growing homeless population as they lose jobs or benefits or become ill and unable to work.

Women and children are the fastest-growing population of homeless people, often because of abusive or economic situations. Many end up living in their cars, like one woman and her daughters in California. They told their story to the television show *America Tonight*:

> For four years, the only life Paula Corb and her two daughters have known is the one inside their 2000 Mazda minivan—stopping once in a while for take-out, groceries and gas…For them, making a pit stop for gas is the equivalent of paying rent. "We go on about a four-block radius," Corb explained. "It's $5 to $10 a day. You see, that's $70 a week times four. I mean, that's more than we really have got." "It was scary. It was depressing," said Alice Corb, 22, the older daughter, of the first night living in the van. "I just kept thinking, 'How could this have possibly happened?' And this mantra in my head just repeated over and over: 'I want to go home.' And I just kept avoiding this one thought in my head that says, 'You don't have a home to go back to.'"

Who's Counting?

How do cities and towns know how many homeless people are living there? Every two years, the federal government mandates a "point in time" survey. On one single night, volunteers and shelter workers search the streets, parks, tunnels, cars, and tents where homeless people might be taking shelter. It is not the best way of collecting data, because a survey that takes place on a cold night, when more homeless people seek shelter inside, won't be as accurate as one that takes place in midsummer. The data that is collected is combined with the number of shelter beds available on that same night to try and see what the success of the previous year's efforts have been to get people off the street and gauge how many people might need shelter in the coming year.

Volunteers often talk to homeless people on the street. They may offer help or gather information, such as to get an estimate of how many homeless live in the city.

According to HUD, homeless people can also be categorized by how long they have been homeless. For example, disabled people who have been continually homeless for a year, or homeless for at least four episodes in three years, are called chronically homeless. "Chronically," a word that refers to something that lasts for a long time and is difficult to get rid of, refers to the fact that they are not just temporarily homeless, but instead are homeless most of the time. There are also chronically homeless families. The chronically homeless are not the largest percentage of the homeless population, but they use more of the available services than people in other homeless categories.

Anyone younger than the age of eighteen who is homeless and without adult supervision is classified as an unaccompanied youth. Those who are younger than the age of twenty and are the parents or legal guardians of young children are referred to as parenting youth, and together they make up a parenting youth household. Young women who become pregnant and give birth while homeless are some of the most vulnerable people in the homeless population. Claireece, who was homeless and pregnant, described her experience to the Healthy Babies Project:

> I was six months pregnant, exploding out of my clothes, and had lost all of my hair. I had lost all hope in myself, others, and even the

world…I grew up with an abusive mother and was used to people shouting, hitting, kicking, and degrading me. After I graduated from high school I moved out. I met a guy that I thought was different…But I soon found out he was abusive and controlling. He would force me to do things that I did not want to, including using drugs…Eventually I fled to friends, only to be thrown out…I took my last bit of money to travel to D.C. to live with a cousin. She too turned me out, explaining her offer of a place to live was "just a joke" and she could not help me.

But despite the classifications that the government assigns to them, someone who is homeless is most likely no different from anyone else. They are more likely to be victims of circumstances that they can't control, which is why homelessness should never be a cause for shame or feeling alone.

Where They Are

Just as there are many different categories of people who become homeless, there are also many different situations that they can find themselves in. HUD divides homelessness into four categories. The first category includes those who are living in a place that

Homeless people, especially teens, may try to live in places that are not meant for human habitation, such as abandoned structures.

is not meant for humans to inhabit, such as bus stations, abandoned buildings, or alleys. It also includes homeless people who are living in emergency shelters, in transitional housing (housing meant to transition them from one situation to another), or people who are leaving prisons, mental health facilities, or other institutions.

The second category of homelessness includes those people who are losing their primary home where they spend days and nights. This might mean that the residence was a hotel or motel or a situation where the person was "doubled up," or living with someone by sleeping on their floor or couch.

The third category is people who live in unstable situations, especially families with children or unaccompanied youth. These situations might include people living in a rental property that is condemned for its uninhabitable conditions or with a family member who might kick them out at any time.

Finally, the fourth category is people who are running from domestic violence situations. They may have escaped violence permanently or are constantly running away from abusive partners who are still trying to find them.

Why They Are

But what are the major reasons why these people find themselves in a homeless situation? According to "Homelessness in America," by the National Coalition for the Homeless, poverty is one of the biggest factors. There are a limited number of affordable housing units and housing assistance programs. The demand for these programs is much greater than the available supply. The mortgage crisis and economic downturn of 2008 also mean that many people defaulted on their mortgages. Unable to make payments, they were evicted. Banks then foreclosed on the homes, meaning that they take over ownership and leave families with nowhere to go. People who live in poverty are also forced to make hard choices about where to spend their money. Even if they have jobs, those jobs may not pay enough to cover housing, food, childcare, health care, and education. Since housing is often the biggest portion of a family's budget, it is often the first thing that must be given up when there isn't enough money. Poverty is on the increase, partly because there is a

Some people find themselves homeless as a result of chronic illness, accidents, or disabilities that prevent them from going to work.

lack of jobs that pay enough to support a family and also because there is a decline in public assistance that would help families with some of their expenses.

There are other factors that contribute to homelessness. If individuals or families can't afford good health care, all it takes is one serious illness, accident, or disability to make it impossible to work. They deplete their savings to pay their medical bills, and eventually they can no longer pay rent or a mortgage and are evicted. Mental illness is also a strong contributor to homelessness, as people who suffer from it often cannot work and don't receive the medical care they need to stabilize their conditions. They may even have a damaged ability to accept help when it is offered. Addiction to drugs or alcohol can also lead to homelessness because an addiction can consume a great deal of money and cause chronic health problems. Addicted people may be in and out of jail, and addiction also makes it difficult to keep a job.

Finally, women who live in poverty, as well as those who live in comfortable homes, may have to choose between themselves and their children being beaten and battered or living on the streets to escape an abusive situation. In many cities, domestic violence is one of the biggest reasons why women and children become homeless. Family relationships can also increase homelessness in other ways, particularly as teens and young adult children begin to rebel or clash with their parents and are either thrown out of their homes or run away to escape them.

Homelessness is a big problem in the United States today, and it is linked to the ups and downs of the economy, the housing market, and the employment market. And while it may seem that most of what is shown in the media about homelessness only concerns those living on city streets or under highway overpass bridges, the truth is that homelessness is taking place everywhere in the country, every day. It is not a reason for shame or for feeling alone. And it is a problem that the United States has grappled with since its founding..

Myths & FACTS

Myth: Homeless people could get jobs, but they just don't want to.

Fact: Of the people living in homeless situations, 44 percent have worked during the previous month, and as many as 25 percent currently have jobs. A job is not a guarantee against homelessness because many jobs simply don't pay enough to survive on. Also, being without a permanent home address and without clean clothes, a computer, a cell phone, and reliable transportation can make it very hard to get a job.

Myth: All homeless people are addicted to drugs and alcohol.

Fact: It is true that 66 percent of the homeless population has a problem with alcohol or drugs. But that leaves a large number of people, both individuals and families, who do not. There are many other reasons for becoming homeless, and being homeless does not automatically mean that people become addicted.

Myth: Homelessness is only a problem in big cities.

Fact: Homelessness is a problem everywhere, from large cities to suburbs to small towns. It may be more obvious in cities, where homeless people live on the sidewalks and in alleys and doorways, but there are other types of homelessness occurring everywhere.

CHAPTER TWO

Homelessness Through History

Homelessness is not a modern problem. Throughout US history, there have always been people who could not afford a place to call home. Sometimes they received help from their communities, but at others times they were left to manage as best they could.

In the earliest days of the United States, before the Revolutionary War, being poor was considered a character flaw. It was supposedly experienced by people who weren't "good," and so God was not providing the means for them to take care of themselves. Poor people who needed help from their communities had to "prove" that they were worth helping, or else they had to move to another

During the Colonial era, it was thought that poor people were not good, which was why they were homeless and unable to care for themselves.

town. Unfortunately, the attitude that homeless people were not good people has still carried over into today, with the idea that they simply need to pick themselves up and get jobs in order to succeed in society.

Auctioning the Poor

In Colonial America, the support of poor people was the responsibility of the town that they lived in, rather than state or federal government. The law said that no individual or family could be left to starve. A town might provide funds for poor families to keep living in their own homes or in rented rooms or houses. But if that family came to the point where they could no longer maintain their own home, even with the town's help, then the next step was to find them a place to live by auctioning them off. During the town's annual town meeting, which was a form of democratic government in the towns of New England, the name of the head of the impoverished family was brought up in front of the town. It was noted how many people were in the family and what their ages were. Once they had this information, the male voting residents of the town would bid on the family's care. This meant that they would present an amount of money that they would be paid by the town in exchange for bringing the poor family into their own home and taking care of them. The lowest bidder would take on the care of that family for the next year. Unfortunately, this system meant that poor families often lived in terrible conditions and did not have enough to eat. Eventually, towns replaced the auctioning off of the poor with the creation of "poor farms," farms that the town maintained where the poor would live and work.

Veterans and Victims

A new kind of homelessness came from the Industrial Revolution. As people began leaving farms and rural areas to find jobs in the cities and their factories, they often had no place to live. Often, going to jail was the only way to find shelter and food. Factory work also brought with it greater possibilities for injury and death because there were few safety regulations or precautions. Workers who were badly hurt or disabled had no safety net to rely on, and if they died, their widows and children would be left without any means of support. They might be evicted from their homes, and it was also a time when parents or other providers began to kick teens and young adults out of their homes because they could not afford to care for them.

Character
Genericus.

Papaver Somniferum. White Poppy

Drug abuse, such as addiction to opium (produced from the poppy plant), created a class of people who could not work and became homeless.

The Civil War brought more homelessness with it. Many homes were destroyed in the South during the war. Medical science had also progressed to the point where badly injured men could survive but be too maimed or disabled to work. They often suffered from what is now called post-traumatic stress disorder (PTSD). The painkiller morphine had also been discovered and was easily available, bringing with it one of the first types of addiction. This epidemic of drug abuse led to the first criminalization of drug addiction, as well as creating a group of people whose addictions prevented them from living normal lives and supporting themselves.

Finally, a series of natural disasters took place between the end of the Civil War and the Great Depression, including the Great Chicago Fire, the 1906 San Francisco earthquake, the flooding of the Mississippi River, and droughts. All of these disasters affected homelessness either by totally destroying homes or livelihoods or by leaving victims disabled and with no resources for survival.

Hands Across America

On May 25, 1986, people all over the United States joined hands in a human chain of 4,000 that stretched from New York City to Los Angeles. Hands Across America was an event intended to call attention to the problem of homelessness and raise money for Americans who were hungry and had no homes. The event did not raise as much money as hoped, and the chain of humans had large gaps in it, but it did raise $15 million. Five million people participated in the chain, and the last ones in the chain in New York City were a family of seven who were living in a homeless shelter.

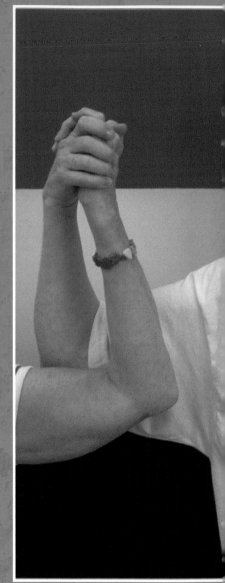

Hands Across America, when millions of people joined hands to create a chain across the country, was an event intended to draw attention to the plight of the homeless.

Depressions, Great and Small

In 1929, the United States entered a period known as the Great Depression, an economic crisis that lasted until World War II. During that time, unemployment was as high as 25 percent, meaning that one in four people did not have a job. As a result, many people could not pay their bills, including rent, mortgages, and taxes, and found themselves homeless. Some moved in with relatives, while others "squatted" in abandoned buildings, meaning that they lived in places without permission. Some homeless individuals and families built shanties out of whatever materials they could scavenge, such as scraps of wood and metal. Whole communities of these shanties were built. These areas became known as Hoovervilles because many people felt that President Hoover was responsible for the economic crisis that had occurred.

In the 1960s and 1970s, a contributor to homelessness was a trend toward deinstitutionalizing mentally ill people. Many were discharged from mental health institutions and treatment centers. Many of these patients did not receive enough follow-up community-based care after their release, and they often became homeless because of their illnesses and their inability to cope. Even today, mentally ill people make up 30 to 50 percent of the homeless population, a much larger percentage than any other category of homeless individuals.

Finally, those who grew up in poverty are said to be living in generational poverty. They have never known any other life, and since their families have been poor for many generations, there are no resources or support to receive further education and move out of poverty. These families get stuck in a cycle of poverty that often leads to homelessness.

A History of Trying to Help

While homelessness has been present throughout American history, there have also been many attempts to help the homeless. In 1948, the United Nations adopted the Universal Declaration of Human Rights. Article 25 of the declaration reads: "Everyone has the right to a standard of living adequate for the health and well-being of himself and of his family, including food, clothing, housing and medical care and necessary social services, and the right to security in the event of unemployment, sickness, disability, widowhood, old age or other lack of livelihood in circumstances beyond his control." One hundred and fifty-five nations ratified the declaration, essentially declaring that they believed that having a home was a basic human right.

From Homeless to Famous

Many famous celebrities and entrepreneurs have had periods of homelessness before they became successful or famous. The singer Jewel was homeless after losing her job because she refused her boss's advances. Comic Jim Carrey's family once lived in a camper, and then in a tent on his sister's lawn. Daniel Craig, the actor who plays James Bond, slept on park benches in London when he was a struggling actor. Even the millionaire financial adviser Suze Orman once lived in her van because she couldn't afford to rent a place to live.

Daniel Craig, who is famous for his movie role as James Bond, was once homeless and had to sleep on park benches.

In 1968, the United States Congress passed a bill for an addition to the Civil Rights Act of 1964. The addition was known as the Fair Housing Act, and it prohibited discrimination in renting or selling housing based on race, gender, color, religion, or national origin. The act was intended to help people secure housing when they may previously have been rejected from renting or owning their own home.

One of the most important steps toward helping the homeless was the McKinney-Vento Act of 1987. This was the first piece of legislation specifically created to address the problem of homelessness. Before it, most of the response to homelessness was created on a local level, but people around the country began advocating for national attention to the problem. In 1986, the Homeless Persons' Survival Act was introduced in Congress. It included preventative actions, emergency measures, and long-term solutions to the problem of homelessness. However, only parts of the act ever became law: an act that no longer required someone to have a home address to receive benefits, and an act that created the Emergency Shelter Grants program and a transitional housing program, both of which were run by the Department of Housing and Urban Development (HUD). Finally, in 1986, the first part of the Homeless Persons' Survival Act finally passed, renamed the

McKinney-Vento Act after the two congressmen who had led the fight for the act. It contains nine sections, called titles, which cover issues such as emergency shelters, transitional housing, health care, education, job training, and some permanent housing. It has been amended four times to add to or modify the original titles.

Homelessness in Modern America

Many people who are homeless today owe their circumstances to the mortgage crisis that began in 2007. The crisis happened because too many people, including those who really couldn't afford a mortgage, were borrowing money to buy homes. Everyone assumed that housing prices would only go up, so buying a house would mean making a profit if it was sold a few years later. People who already had mortgages were taking out second mortgages and using the money for whatever they wanted, and yet the wages for most jobs were not going up. When housing prices stopped rising and interest rates on certain kinds of mortgages rose, many people could no longer afford their payments. Banks foreclosed on their homes, and soon there were too many empty bank-owned houses. Banks and investors began to fail because they had lent too much money. At the same time, the US economy

As a result of the mortgage crisis that began in 2007, many families lost their homes to foreclosure and became homeless.

was no longer growing, and prices for everything were rising. Many people lost their homes to foreclosure and became homeless. Though some may still have had jobs, they were now unable to afford their homes.

The lingering effects of the mortgage crisis and the economic recession that followed have contributed to the numbers of people who are homeless. However, some homeless people are in that situation through no real fault of their own: they are known as unaccompanied youth.

CHAPTER THREE

Homelessness and Teens

It's easy to think of homeless people as being mostly adult men, but the truth is that every year, two million teens will be homeless at some point. This category of the homeless population is known as unaccompanied youth. They may be younger than eighteen, or between eighteen and twenty-four, but they live alone, outside of a family, and are not accompanied by a parent or guardian.

Justin, a twenty-year-old, lives alone on the streets. His story, as he told it to Covenant House, is a familiar one for homeless teens:

> People tell me to go home, to get a job. I can't go home. I was abandoned by my mother and disowned by my father. I have no one but myself. But I'm so tired. I've been doing this for two years. I bet most people would lose their minds out here after three weeks. I can't get a job because I don't have a home. You need an address to

While the media often portrays homeless people as adults, the teen homelessness statistics are shocking: two million teens become homeless every year.

send your paycheck. I wish I could tell a boss to send my paycheck to the alley but it doesn't work like that. I just wish that people would understand that when they walk by a street kid, it could have been them, or their own kid. Just because we're on the street doesn't mean we're not human.

Unaccompanied youth make up as much as 30 percent of the total homeless population. So why are there so many teens and young adults living without permanent homes?

The Official Definition

According to the McKinney-Vento Act, the official definition of the term "homeless children and youth" is as follows:

A.
means individuals who lack a fixed, regular, and adequate nighttime residence...; and

B.

includes —

i.

children and youths who are sharing the housing of other persons due to loss of housing, economic hardship, or a similar reason; are living in motels, hotels, trailer parks, or camping grounds due to the lack of alternative adequate accommodations; are living in emergency or transitional shelters; are abandoned in hospitals; or are awaiting foster care placement;

ii.

children and youths who have a primary nighttime residence that is a public or private place not designed for or ordinarily used as a regular sleeping accommodation for human beings...

iii.

children and youths who are living in cars, parks, public spaces, abandoned buildings, substandard housing, bus or train stations, or similar settings; and

iv.
migratory children who qualify as homeless

It's All Connected

The reasons why teens find themselves homeless fall into three categories, which are all connected. Teen homelessness can be caused by family problems, economic problems, and unstable housing situations.

Family problems can cover a wide range of situations. Teens may experience physical or emotional abuse from a parent or a parent's partner until they reach the point where they run away either for self-preservation or because they can no longer tolerate the abuse. A study by the US Department of Health and Human Services found that 46 percent of runaway and homeless youth had been physically abused and 17 percent had experienced unwanted sexual activity by a family or household member. Drug and alcohol addiction also play a major role in driving teens from their homes or as a reason why parents become abusive. Often, an addicted parent will be arrested and

Teens who rebel against parental authority may find themselves being kicked out of their own homes and forced to fend for themselves.

incarcerated, leaving teens with no means of support. Addicted parents or caregivers may also neglect children and teens in their care, failing to provide enough food or clothing or a safe place to live.

Being a teenager or young adult means seeking independence and questioning authority, and in most families, this is a natural process that parents and teens work through together. But teens who rebel against their parents' authority might also find that they are no longer welcome in their own home. These strained family relationships may lead to a teen being kicked out by parents, running away from rebellion, or a desire for independence and freedom of choice. One former homeless teen, Julie, described her experience on the Covenant House website: "Things used to be ok, but then my father lost his job a few years ago and he went kind of crazy. Ever since then, he's been manic and angry." She continued to explain how she came home from school one day and her father "had snapped." Julie was told that he would no longer take care of her. Her father told her that if she was smart, she could survive on her own. Her father dumped all her clothes on the sidewalk and said not to come back. Julie knocked and knocked on the door, begging her stepmother to let her in, but she told Julie to leave. She spent the night on a bench in the park, hoping that it would all blow over by morning. It didn't. Julie was turned away by her own parents.

Another issue that drives teens and young adults from their homes is sexual orientation. LGBTQ+ (lesbian, gay, bisexual, transgender, or questioning) teens often face negative reactions from their families to their sexual identity, often to the point where they become completely alienated and either leave home or are kicked out. It is estimated that LGBTQ+ teens make up between 20 and 40 percent of all homeless youth. At a time when they are struggling to find themselves, these teens may be forced from their homes because of the choices they make.

How Old Is Too Old?

In most states, when teens turn eighteen, they have aged out of the foster care system and are often abruptly turned out of whatever foster home they are living in. If they have no permanent family of their own to return to, they are suddenly expected to take care of themselves, often without the resources and skills they need to do so and with no safety net. More than twenty thousand teens age out of foster care every year. They are less likely than the general population of teens to graduate from high school and are less likely to attend college.

Dollars and Cents

Another factor that families may struggle with, and one that often leads to teen homelessness, is money. Many families are facing home foreclosure, bankruptcy, huge amounts of debt, and unemployment. A family's economic circumstances can lead to situations where teens become a burden. The wages of the working adults may be too low to live on, or if the family receives benefits like welfare, they might be insufficient. Death or job loss can also devastate a family's finances. If a family lives in poverty, they may tell their teens to move out when they reach the age of eighteen, simply because they cannot afford another person to feed, shelter, and clothe. Eighteen-year-olds may be considered old enough to fend for themselves, but this often disrupts their chances for a good education. Some teens are kicked out by their parents because they have mental health issues that the family

Losing a home and being forced to move out, often to live on the streets, is a traumatic experience for every member of a family.

cannot afford to treat. Even teens with solid family relationships may become homeless along with their parents, but then leave to go off on their own.

Teens who have been incarcerated in a juvenile detention facility for committing crimes, in mental health institutions, or in the foster care system may become homeless when they are released from these kinds of institutions at the age of eighteen. This is referred to as "aging out" because once they reach this age, they are no longer considered to be minors and are no longer eligible for programs that help children. Foster children, in particular, may be brutally ripped from lives where they have been going to school and doing well. According to Foster Club, Nicole, a former foster child, remembered, "I turned 18 a month before I graduated from high school. The day after graduation, I was kicked out of my foster home, where I had been living for two years. I was 18, a high school graduate on my way to college in the fall, and I was homeless." Foster kids who age out of the system also lose their support system of adults and family at a critical time in their lives, which can have drastic consequences. As stated by Foster Club, the statistics for teens aging out of foster care are grim:

• One in four will be incarcerated within the first two years after they leave the system.

One in four foster kids will find themselves in prison within the first two years after they leave foster care.

- More than one-fifth will become homeless at some time after age eighteen.
- Approximately 58 percent had a high school degree at age nineteen, compared to 87 percent of a national comparison group of non-foster youth.
- Of youth who aged out of foster care and are older than the age of twenty-five, fewer than 3 percent earned their college degrees, compared with 28 percent of the general population. Transitions are even more difficult for teens released from juvenile detention or a mental health facility because they are often not prepared to survive on their own after years of being sheltered and fed.

Consequences of Teen Homelessness

Teens face many problems when they become homeless, whether they are living in a shelter or on the street. Mental health issues are common, such as anxiety and depression, as well as low self-esteem. Teens may act out with abusive behaviors, like self-harming (cutting, self-tattooing, or burning), or even attempt

Homeless young women have higher rates of unintended pregnancies than the general population due to lack of access to health care and birth control.

suicide. These issues, as well as stress and desperation, can lead to substance abuse with alcohol or drugs. Homeless teens may also commit crimes to survive or become victims of crimes themselves because they are vulnerable. Others resort to prostitution and unsafe sexual practices. This kind of "survival sex" means they are trading sex for money, shelter, or drugs. It can lead to diseases and pregnancy, especially with a lack of access to birth control or health care, and homeless teens have a higher rate of pregnancy than the general population. Other health problems related to homelessness include poor nutrition and untreated illnesses, as well as HIV and AIDS. And death is always a possibility from any of these factors.

Finally, homeless teens usually cannot attend school and have little chance of pursuing higher education. This means that they are automatically limited as to their choices in the future and in their ability to get a well-paying job and climb out of their circumstances.

For teens and young adults, the "unaccompanied youth" of the homeless statistics, it can be very difficult to cope with their circumstances alone. They need practical help, right away.

CHAPTER FOUR

Help for the Homeless

It is difficult to be homeless no matter how old you are or what your circumstances might be. But for teens, in particular, homelessness requires a set of coping skills that they may never have developed. If the transition from a normal life of going to school, hanging out with friends, and returning to a stable home is suddenly swept away, it can feel like everything has changed and there are few resources for survival. Even school may seem like a haven. According to an article by Raychelle Cassada Lohmann, "Finally the bell rang and school was over. Students gathered their materials and excitedly scampered into the hallways...All of the students were eager to exit the building anticipating the long weekend; that is all but one, Jeremy. Jeremy relished the comfort of the school building. It was the only place in his life that provided safety, security and stability. You

When the weather is good, homeless people may construct their own shelters and camps under bridges or in other public areas.

see, like thousands of today's teens, Jeremy was homeless. His weekend would consist of trying to find a place to stay that provided shelter, warmth and food." The basic needs of life that may once have been taken for granted are suddenly much more difficult to access. According to the blog Survival Guide for Homelessness: "I want you to think about your troubles one at a time. You must address the same needs an adult has, but you must do it with fewer social resources." So where can a newly homeless teen go for help?

Looking for Shelter

Shelter is the most important thing for a homeless teen to find. The best place to start is close to home: find a relative or a friend who will provide a place to stay, even if just temporarily. Even a college-aged friend who will share a dorm room or a couch in an apartment is a better option than being on the streets. It is important, in the case of staying with a teenaged friend, that their parents are aware of the homeless teen's presence and agree to it. Teens who belong to a church may also find that it provides resources for people who need to find shelter.

Finding food is a necessity, but it can often be difficult. Many churches offer free meals to homeless and poverty-stricken people living in their area.

If staying with relatives or friends is not an option, teens can look for open beds at a shelter or pay a minimal amount to stay in a youth hostel or a YMCA. Teens with cars may have to live in them temporarily, but if they are forced to live on the streets, public places like libraries, bus stations, and transportation centers are warmer and safer than the street. Riding a subway or bus is also a way to stay warm for a while. Warehouses and abandoned buildings should be considered a last resort as a place to take shelter. Camping in a tent in a park or other public outside area is an option during warmer weather. Avoid any arrangement in which staying with someone is in exchange for sex or other favors.

Finding Food and More

For homeless teens who are still enrolled in school, it is likely that they can be enrolled in free breakfast and lunch programs, giving them at least two solid meals a day. Other options include going to soup kitchens and free meal programs sponsored by homeless shelters or food pantries. Some teens will panhandle, meaning that they ask for donations from people on the street and use that money to purchase food. "Dumpster diving" for discarded food behind restaurants is not safe because spoiled food can cause illness, and most homeless teens cannot easily get medical care.

Health on the Streets

In San Francisco, a mobile teen health van, sponsored by the Lucile Packard Children's Hospital Stanford and the Children's Health Fund, brings medical services to homeless teens around the city. The van's staff includes a doctor specializing in adolescent medicine, a nurse practitioner, a social worker, a dietitian, and a registrar/driver. The van provides physical exams and treatment, illness and injury care, pregnancy tests, birth control, and counseling for substance abuse, mental health, and nutrition. They can also provide referrals to social service agencies that offer help to the homeless. All of these services are free of charge. Since the service started in 1996, it has had more than fifteen thousand visits.

Schools are also useful for personal hygiene because locker rooms usually have shower facilities. Many shelters and assistance organizations provide free toiletries to the homeless, and some shelters may allow them to use shower facilities even if they do not stay there. Clothing, which is vital for staying warm

Miracle Messages

In December of 2014, Kevin Adler was walking down the street in San Francisco, handing out hot tea and biscuits to homeless people and asking them if they had any family or friends that they wanted to record a message for. He was doing this in honor of his uncle, Mark, who had suffered from schizophrenia and spent thirty years on and off the streets. Out of this was born a service called Miracle Messages, which records short messages from homeless people to their often long-lost relatives. A global network of volunteers delivers the messages using social media. Most of the recipients are happy to receive the messages, and 40 percent of them have resulted in family reunions or stable housing situations for the homeless message giver. It also helps them reconnect with their support system.

in colder climates, is often also available from shelters and clothing donation organizations. Churches may also provide used clothing and warm coats.

Medical care can be more difficult to find. Many towns and cities maintain free clinics where homeless people can walk in and receive care. Some cities are

Homelessness is more difficult for teens than for adults because teens lack experience and are more vulnerable as a result of their age.

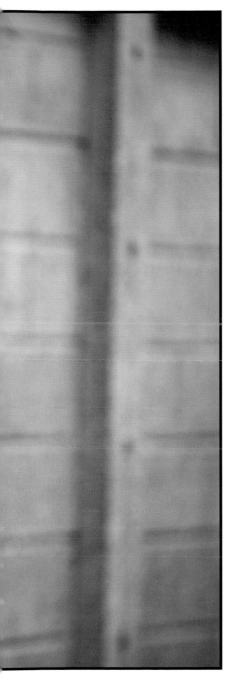

starting to have mobile vans that provide free medical care at various places each day, on a schedule that allows for follow-up care from one week to the next.

Finally, it is important to maintain contact. Social media is a good tool for staying in touch with friends and family and can be accessed from free library computers. A cell phone is very valuable because it also provides a stable phone number to use when looking for a job, as well as access to teen homelessness hotlines.

Being homeless as a teen is more difficult than being a homeless adult because age and inexperience will make many things more difficult. Teens are much more vulnerable than adults, and there are many things they can't do simply because they are not legally old enough. But teens can survive homelessness and move onto more stable, fulfilling lives. According to "A Message to Homeless Teens" on the Survival Guide to Homelessness website: "The most important thing I can teach is that this will change. Things will get better. Have fun every day. It will help you think. Do something silly. Each day you will find new solutions. Beware of people who want to take over responsibility for your life. What they offer is seldom worth what they want in return."

CHAPTER FIVE

What Can Be Done?

ome people are homeless by choice, but many others are homeless because of circumstances they can't control. Homeless people are in almost every city, town, and suburb across the United States. Sometimes they are obvious, and sometimes they are not. No matter where they are, or what their situation is, however, homeless people can benefit from the help of those around them who aren't homeless. Even if the presence of homeless people makes others uncomfortable, there are ways to interact positively and provide help if wanted.

This café in Grand Junction, Colorado, supports the local homeless teenage residents of a neighborhood shelter by providing them with employment.

Teens Helping Teens

Teens, in particular, may want to help other teens who are homeless, especially if they are friends or classmates. The first step is identifying teens who might be homeless, even if they don't want to admit it. Teens want to fit in and may feel that homelessness is something to be ashamed or embarrassed about, so they may try to hide the signs. At school, they may suddenly be absent regularly or just stop coming to school entirely. They may not be as clean as usual, either in their personal hygiene or their clothing. They may develop serious health or dental issues that aren't dealt with. The quality of their schoolwork may also fall without any explanation. Socially, they may no longer want to hang out in the usual places or do anything after school; or they may be reluctant to leave school or leave a friend's house when they normally would. It also helps to pay close attention to conversations because

Volunteers from teen outreach organizations often visit known locations where homeless teens camp, leaving food, clothing, blankets, and other necessities.

a group of friends might be creating a schedule of homes for a homeless friend to stay in. Teens, or their teachers, who suspect that friends or students might be homeless should make sure that they offer—or at least mention—resources and people for them to contact for help. Teens can offer their friend a temporary place to stay, ask for help on his or her behalf, contact help lines, and assist their friend in finding resources.

On the street, it can be difficult to tell if teens are homeless, because unlike homeless adults, they don't usually spend time in the same places every day. They don't always like to admit to being homeless and would rather blend in with their peers and friends and seem like everyone else.

An Experiment

The New York City Rescue Mission conducted an experiment for a campaign called "Make Them Visible," to show how invisible most homeless people are to the people who pass them on a daily basis. They hired actors for a documentary film, but they also contacted family members of the actors to see if they would be willing to dress up as homeless people. They did not tell the actors, who walked along streets and came face to face with their relatives. They did not recognize their relatives as they walked past them, simply because they were dressed and acted as homeless people. The actors were later shown the video footage of themselves walking past their relatives without even realizing it. "The experiment is a powerful reminder that the homeless are people, just like us, with one exception," Craig Mayes, executive director of New York City Rescue Mission. "They are in trouble and in pain. And they are someone's uncle or cousin or wife."

Offering Help on the Street

What are the best ways to help the homeless people who are on the street every day? Surprisingly, one of the biggest things is to acknowledge the presence of homeless people and engage with them in a casual conversation. Homelessness can be corrosive to a person's self-worth, and it can be very lonely, too. Often, a simple hello in passing can make a big difference in a person's day. For more tangible help, experts say that it's usually best to give gift cards for grocery stores or fast food restaurants, rather than cash. Small, nutritional food items like granola bars, as well as bottles of water, are also useful. Even buying a second cup of coffee in the morning and giving it to someone on the street is a gesture that is helpful.

In cold weather climates, it can also be helpful to give out warm clothing. It doesn't have to be new, but it could be serviceable clothing that is no longer useful or is the wrong size or color. In warm weather climates, clean T-shirts and sun hats can make a big difference. Also, small-sized toiletries from hotels are also useful for people living on the street.

One user on Reddit, a social media news website, asked for comments from formerly homeless people, asking how people could best help the homeless. One

One of the best ways to help the homeless is to volunteer at local soup kitchens that serve meals to homeless people.

user responded: "When people ask homeless what do you need, they are thinking about objects, things like hats, socks and gloves or any other things useful in routine life. These objects make a small difference. But the most important things are not objects. Things that make most impact and help someone are non-objects. Dignity. Kindness and understanding. Encouragement."

Volunteering

Another way to help the homeless is by volunteering for organizations that help them. Soup kitchens, shelters, food pantries, hotline programs, and church groups often need many extra hands, and donating time rather than material objects is a good way to help the homeless. These kinds of organizations are also a good place to donate money because it is more likely to be used to directly help the homeless. Some smaller towns and suburbs might also maintain special funds to quietly provide assistance to homeless citizens or people in danger of becoming homeless, and they also welcome donations.

If there aren't any organizations that help the homeless in a particular area, then it could be a good idea to start one. Teens can start projects in their schools or churches to collect used clothing or personal hygiene kits, or hold food drives for shelters and soup kitchens. They can also hold benefits to raise money for homeless organizations.

Helping Hands

There are many organizations that help homeless teens and runaways that have branches in most major cities around the United States and Canada. They include Covenant House, StandUp for Kids, National Network for Youth (NN4Y), and the Family and Youth Services Bureau of the US Government. In addition, many major cities also have their own organizations for helping the homeless. These organizations can be found online, but for homeless teens, their information may also be posted in public areas. Some organizations even run vans that drive through city streets at night, offering food, blankets, and places to stay.

What NOT to Do

There are some things that people should not do when it comes to interacting with homeless people, especially on the street. They should not ignore them, even when they are asked for money. Homeless people may have already given up a great deal of pride to ask strangers for money, and by ignoring them, it perpetuates the feeling that homeless people are invisible to everyone else. It's better simply to say, "I'm sorry, I can't today." Never tell a homeless person to go get a job—many homeless people actually do have jobs, but their jobs don't pay enough for them to have housing. Never assume that someone sitting on the street asking for money is lying, even though some people think that homeless people get up at the end of the day and go home to comfortable houses. And never assume that homeless people are all criminals and drug users.

In the end, not all homeless people are the same or homeless for the same reasons. And while it is necessary to be careful when interacting with any stranger, it is also necessary to show basic human courtesy. Ed, a homeless man from London, summed it up an article by Nick Hilton: "You've just got to try to make people aware of why you got out here. I've got a degree in psychology, so I'm good at working people out. You've got to do that so that they can understand.

Homeless people have already given up their pride to ask for help on the streets and should at least be acknowledged.

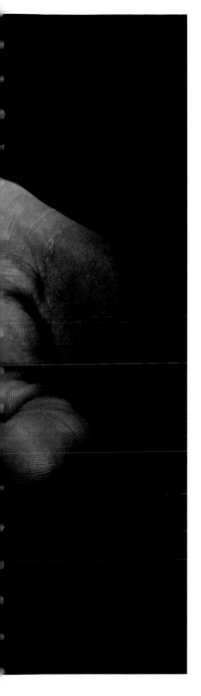

When they see what I've gone through, people often ask me, 'How did you survive it?' But, put simply, you've got to."

Homelessness is an issue that isn't going to go away, whether it concerns adults, unaccompanied teens, or families with children. But there are things that homeless people, especially teens, can do to start making their way out of homelessness.

CHAPTER SIX

Moving Beyond Homelessness

Homelessness, especially for those who find themselves in that situation, may seem like the end of the line. But it does not have to be. There are many people who move back out of homelessness and many organizations and resources to help them achieve that goal.

A Success Story

Dawn Loggins had just spent six weeks at a summer course for gifted students and was about to enter her senior year of high school when her parents abandoned her. Vivian Kuo described the story:

> [Dawn] kept calling her parents' phone, only to learn it had been disconnected. "When I returned, my grandmother had been dropped off at a

Dawn Loggins, abandoned by her parents and left homeless, still managed to excel in school and was accepted at Harvard University.

local homeless shelter, my brother had just left, and my parents had just gone," she says. "I found out later they had moved to Tennessee." Her voice is steady, matter of fact. "I never expected my parents to just, like, leave."

Dawn slept on couches and floors at friends' houses. She didn't want to enter the social services system because she might be uprooted and forced to move around. Dawn was an excellent student and wanted to finish high school in her own school. The faculty at the school rallied around her and found her a place to live and a job as a custodian at the school. She could concentrate on school and her goal of going to college. She applied to five different schools, including Harvard, her dream school.

Months passed. She was accepted to the four schools in North Carolina.

Days went by. Nothing from Harvard.

But on a sunny day earlier this year... there was a letter from Harvard, the type of letter every high school senior dreads from a university—a regular-sized envelope, the ominous sign of rejection. Cautiously, she opened it: "Dear Ms. Loggins, I'm delighted to report that the admissions committee has asked me to inform you that you will be

admitted to the Harvard College class of 2016...
We send such an early positive indication only
to outstanding applicants..."

She gasped when she read those words.

Dawn flourished at Harvard and graduated in May
of 2016. In 2014, *Business Insider* named her one of its "19
Incredibly Impressive Students at Harvard." She also has
a nonprofit organization to benefit other disadvantaged
students and has raised more than $35,000.

Dawn's story is just one of hundreds showing
how homeless teens and adults have found ways to
move out of their circumstances and achieve their
goals. Some are helped by friends and teachers, as
Dawn was, but there are many other resources that
can help homeless people move off the streets and
back into productive, stable lives.

Help From HUD

The United States government, through HUD, has
many programs to help the homeless. The Continuum
of Care (CoC) program promotes community
involvement in helping homeless people and quickly
rehousing them. They provide funding to nonprofits,
as well as state and local governments, to accomplish
this and to help homeless individuals and families
become self-sufficient.

HUD also has an Emergency Shelter Grants program to provide funding for more emergency homeless shelters, as well as the Housing Opportunities for Persons With AIDS (HOPWA) program for people specifically suffering from HIV/AIDS. There is also the Title V program, which allows organizations such as homeless shelters to use surplus federal government property to assist homeless people. On January 13, 2017, HUD announced a new program, the Youth Homelessness Demonstration Program, which will award funding to ten communities that are working to end youth homelessness. HUD also has programs to help people who have become homeless because of the closing of military bases, in addition to a joint program with the US Department of Veterans Affairs to provide housing vouchers and counseling specifically to military veterans, who make up a large portion of the homeless population. While all of HUD's programs are government-based, homeless people can visit their website to locate services available in their area and learn how to access them.

Organizations like the United States Department of Housing and Urban Development (HUD) offer housing assistance programs to help people who have become homeless.

Community organizations often provide meals for local homeless people, like this Thanksgiving dinner at Pine Street Inn, the largest shelter in New England.

Community Help

For many homeless people, however, the most accessible kind of help comes from community organizations. These organizations come in two types: local branches of national (or even international) organizations and organizations that are entirely local and are created and run by local communities. National organizations include the National Coalition for the Homeless, which is "a national network of people who are currently experiencing or who have experienced homelessness, activists and advocates, community based and faith-based service providers, and others committed to a single mission: To prevent and end homelessness while ensuring the immediate needs of those experiencing homelessness are met and their civil rights protected." The National Alliance to End Homelessness, Volunteers of America, Covenant House, and StandUp for Kids are other organizations with branches in many major American cities. There are also national service groups, such as the Lions Club, Kiwanis, or Rotary, that may have programs for helping the homeless.

Local community based programs will vary from place to place. They may be more difficult to find, and it may require calling or visiting a social service agency or a city or town government office to find them. For homeless teens, visiting a school

In situations such as medical emergencies or where there is dangerous or criminal activity taking place, it is always best for homeless people to find a way to call 911.

guidance office is another way to find resources and help. Many churches and synagogues also have outreach programs to help the homeless and the hungry. Again, it might be necessary to visit or call the specific church group and ask if they have assistance, but most clergy members are used to being asked for help and can at least guide homeless people in the right direction to get help.

Emergency Assistance

For homeless people in dire situations who have an emergency medical condition or find themselves in a criminal or dangerous situation, the best thing to do is to call 911. Not only will emergency service personnel help with the immediate problem, but they will also know where to get additional assistance and what organizations and resources are available.

Almost every national and many local organizations dedicated to helping the homeless also have hotlines that are answered twenty-four hours a day. These hotlines can provide immediate help, sometimes even sending out a van or an organization worker to get the homeless person and bring them to a shelter. In major metropolitan areas, these hotline numbers are often posted in places like bus stations and libraries, as well as in phone books (when they are still available). Anyone can find them on a computer in a public library or internet café or by using a cell phone.

It's Always Possible

No matter what their circumstances, homeless individuals and families can always find some sort of help, and it often comes from unexpected sources: the kindness of strangers, not just the work of large organizations. When he was nineteen, Matthew Tejeda found himself checking into a homeless shelter in New York City. His story was told in a *Forbes* magazine article by Micah Solomon: "I carried a key in my pocket when I was homeless because I believed that one day I'd have my own place," he said. He was lucky to apply for a job at a coffee shop and find that the manager was willing to give him a chance, even when he explained that he was living in a shelter. Matthew got the job, but as it did not pay enough for him to afford the high city rents, he continued to live in the

Having a key to one's own place to sleep at night can make all the difference to someone who has been homeless.

shelter for another year, which could be challenging: "One of the real challenges of this, while trying to hold down a job and better yourself, is that the shelter life—sleeping in a room with seven other guys and no enforced sleep schedule—means getting very little sleep. It's hard opening a [coffee] store at 4:30 am off no sleep. Some nights that were really loud at the shelter, rather than lying sleepless in my bed, I'd lock myself in the bathroom for a couple of hours with my head against the wall to try and get a nap in before opening."

Eventually, Matthew was promoted to assistant store manager and, for the first time, could afford his own apartment, with some help from an existing employee assistance fund through his store's parent company: "I got promoted and moved into my apartment in the same week. The first night in my apartment I cried my eyes out. For the first time in my entire life I knew exactly where I would sleep that night and the next

Homelessness can result from circumstances such as war or becoming a refugee. War cost this Yemeni woman her home, so she lives in a tent and begs on the streets.

night after that, and that sense of security did not depend on anything in the world except myself." He has since been made the manager at one of the chain's busiest locations, at New York's Penn Station. Matthew's story shows that someone who is homeless is able to successfully move out of unemployment and a shelter situation and into his own space and a successful life.

Homelessness is not, and never has been, an issue that simply goes away. In fact, with an uncertain economy, it may even become a bigger problem in the near future. It is important not only to recognize homelessness as a problem that needs to be alleviated, but also to remember that homelessness is not a character flaw. Anyone can become homeless at any time. There is no shame in it, and there are many people and organizations that can help. And for those who are fortunate enough to not experience homelessness, there will always be many ways to help those who are.

10 Great Questions to Ask a Homelessness Social Worker

1. Where can a homeless person find out about resources and organizations that will help?

2. Can homeless people hold jobs?

3. Are homeless teens allowed to remain in school?

4. What should a homeless person do if he or she feels unsafe or threatened?

5. How does the legal system handle homeless people?

6. Do homeless people have the right to live on the streets?

7. Is it illegal to panhandle for money?

8. Are there special shelters and organizations for homeless teens?

9. What is the first thing someone should do when they become homeless?

10. What can I do to help homeless people in my area?

Glossary

abusive Engaging in violence or cruelty, either physically or verbally.

addiction The compulsive need for a substance like drugs or alcohol.

bankruptcy The state of being unable to repay debts.

bipolar disorder A mental illness characterized by alternating periods of extreme happiness and extreme depression.

budget An estimate of the income and expenses available for a certain period of time.

chronic Constantly reoccurring or lasting a long time.

condemn To judge a building as being unfit or even dangerous to live in or use.

criminalization Turning an activity into a criminal offense by making it illegal.

democratic Based on a form of government where people choose leaders by voting.

deplete To use up a supply of something, such as money.

domestic Having to do with a household or family relationships.

economic Relating to the earning, distribution, and use of money.

eligible Qualified to participate in or be chosen for something.

episode An incident, event, or series of events.

evict To remove someone from land or a building, often with the support of the law.

flaw A defect or imperfection.

generational Relating to the different generations of a particular family.

guardian Someone who is legally responsible for the care of another person.

hygiene A practice that has to do with staying clean and healthy.

legislation A law or set of laws made by a government.

makeshift Something that is temporary or of low quality but used because of a sudden need.

mandate An official order to do something.

mortgage A long-term loan from a bank used to purchase a house.

preconception An idea or opinion that someone has before learning about something directly.

ratify To make something official by signing a contract or voting.

schizophrenia A mental illness that affects how a person thinks, feels, and behaves.

shanty A small, crudely built shack, usually made of found materials.

transitional Having to do with a period or process of transition.

uninhabitable A place that is unsuitable to live in.

Coalition for the Homeless

129 Fulton Street

New York, NY 10038

(212) 776-2000

Website: http://www.coalitionforthehomeless.org

Facebook: @nyhomeless

Twitter: @NYHomeless

Instagram: @nyhomeless

The Coalition for the Homeless assists the homeless through direct programs for food and clothing, as well as by working with legal and government systems on behalf of the homeless.

Covenant House

Covenant House Headquarters

461 Eighth Avenue

New York, NY 10001

(800) 388-3888

Website: https://www.covenanthouse.org

Facebook: @CovenantHouse

Twitter: @CovenantHouse

With branch houses located in twenty-seven cities in the United States, as well as Canada and Latin America, Covenant House is specifically dedicated to helping homeless and runaway teens.

Family Promise

71 Summit Avenue

Summit, NJ 07901

(908) 273-1100

Website: https://familypromise.org

Facebook: @FamilyPromise

Twitter: @fpnational

Instagram: @family.promise

The mission of Family Promise is to help homeless and low-income families achieve lasting independence through community based help.

The Homeless Charity

15 Broad Street

Akron, OH 44305

(330) 416-7519

Website: www.thehomelesscharity.org

Facebook: @the homelesscharity

Twitter: @sagerock

The Homeless Charity assist the homeless with practical services, such as laundry and showers, as well as job and housing assistance.

National Alliance to End Homelessness

1518 K Street NW, 2nd Floor

Washington, DC 20005

(202) 638-1526

Website: http://www.endhomelessness.org

Facebook: @naehomelessness

Twitter: @naehomelessness

The alliance works toward ending homelessness
by improving homelessness policies, building
resources for helping the homeless, and
educating the public and political leaders.

National Coalition for the Homeless

2201 P Street NW

Washington, DC 20037

(202) 462-4822

Website: http://nationalhomeless.org

Facebook: @NationalCoalitionfortheHomeless

Twitter: @Ntl_Homeless

The National Coalition for the Homeless is a
national network of homeless people, activists,
advocates, community and faith-based service
providers, and others committed to ending
homelessness.

Raising the Roof

263 Eglinton Avenue West, Suite 200

Toronto, ON M4R 1B1

Canada

(416) 481-1838

Website: http://www.raisingtheroof.org

Facebook: @RaisingtheRoof

Twitter: @RaisingTheRoof

Instagram: @RaisingTheRoof

This organization works with local agencies all across Canada to find long-term solutions to the problem of homelessness.

True Colors Fund

330 West 38th Street, Suite 405

New York, NY 10018

(212) 461-4401

Website: https://truecolorsfund.org

Facebook: @truecolorsfund

Twitter: @TrueColorsFund

The True Colors Fund works to end homelessness among lesbian, gay, bisexual, and transgender youth, creating a world in which all young people can be their true selves.

Youth Without Shelter

6 Warrendale Court

Toronto, ON M9V 1P9

Canada

(416) 748-0110

Website: http://www.yws.on.ca

Facebook: @ywstoronto

Twitter: @YWSToronto

Instagram: @ywstoronto

Youth Without Shelter is a referral and support service and emergency shelter for Canadians ages sixteen to twenty-four living in the Toronto area.

Websites

Because of the changing nature of Internet links, Rosen Publishing has developed an online list of websites related to the subject of this book. This site is updated regularly. Please use this link to access this list:

http://www.rosenlinks.com/COP/Home

For Further Reading

Brenner, Summer. *Ivy, Homeless in San Francisco.* Oakland CA: PM Press, 2011.

Burnes, Donald W. *Ending Homelessness: Why We Haven't, How We Can.* Boulder, CO: Lynne Rienner Publishers, 2016.

Desmond, Matthew. *Evicted: Poverty and Profit in the American City.* New York, NY: Crown Publishing, 2016.

Edin, Kathryn J. *$2.00 a Day: Living on Almost Nothing in America.* New York, NY: Houghton Mifflin, 2015.

Graham, Alan. *Welcome Homeless: One Man's Journey of Discovering the Meaning of Home.* New York, NY: Thomas Nelson, 2017.

Hubbard, Jim. *Lives Turned Upside Down: Homeless Children in Their Own Words and Photographs.* New York, NY: Aladdin Books, 2007.

Kennedy, Michelle. *Without a Net: Middle Class and Homeless (with Kids) in America.* New York, NY: Penguin Books, 2006.

Kozol, Jonathan. *Rachel and Her Children: Homeless Families in America.* New York, NY: Broadway Books, 2006.

Lüsted, Marcia Amidon. *I Am Homeless. Now What?* New York, NY: Rosen Publishing, 2017.

Padgett, Deborah. *Housing First: Ending Homelessness, Transforming Systems, and*

Changing Lives. New York, NY: Oxford University Press, 2015.

Ross, Anthony D. *Homeless at Age 13 to a College Graduate: An Autobiography*. Manila, Philippines: Step One Publishing, 2014.

Ryan, Kevin, and Tina Kelley. *Almost Home: Helping Kids Move from Homelessness to Hope*. New York, NY: Wiley, 2012.

Van Draanen, Wendelin. *Runaway*. New York, NY: Ember Publishing, 2012.

Wasserman, Jason Adam. *At Home on the Street: People, Poverty, and a Hidden Culture of Homelessness*. Boulder, CO: Lynne Rienner Publishers, 2009.

Bibliography

"11 Homeless People Who Became Rich And Famous." Business Insider. Retrieved March 17, 2017. http://www.businessinsider.com/formerly-homeless-people-who-became-famous-2012-6#oscar-winner-halle-berry-once-stayed-in-a-homeless-shelter-in-her-early-twenties-1.

Cawthon, Graham. "How Is the 'Homeless to Harvard Girl' Doing 2 Years Later? Just Fine." Shelbystar.com, September 14, 2015. http://www.shelbystar.com/20140915/how-is-the-homeless-to-harvard-girl-doing-2-years-later-just-fine/309159820.

"Children and Youth Experiencing Homelessness: An Introduction to the Issues." National Center for Homeless Education, Winter 2014. http://nche.ed.gov/downloads/briefs/introduction.pdf.

Demetrius, Dina. "Mobile Homes: Many 'Hidden Homeless' Americans Living in Vehicles." *America Tonight*, October 10, 2014. http://america.aljazeera.com/watch/shows/america-tonight/articles/2014/10/10/mobile-homes-manyhiddenhomelessamericanslivinginvehicles.html.

Desmond, Matthew. *Evicted: Poverty and Profit in the American City*. New York, NY: Crown Publishers, 2016.

Dowd, Katie. "What's the best way to help the homeless? Former homeless people share their advice." SF Gate, November 23, 2016. http://www.sfgate.com/news/article/best-ways-to-help-homeless-advice-sf-10631036.php.

Fischler, Robert. "The History of Homelessness in America 1640s to Present." Downtown Congregations to End Homelessness, November 16, 2011. http://www.dceh.org/the-history-of-homelessness-in-america-1640s-to-present/.

Gates, Sara. "People Disguised As Homeless Ignored By Loved Ones On Street In Stunning Social Experiment." Huffington Post, April 24, 2014. http://www.huffingtonpost.com/2014/04/23/make-them-visible-homeless-video_n_5200574.html.

Hilton, Nick. "How to Treat the Homeless: Tips from Actual Homeless People." Vice, May 6, 2015. https://www.vice.com/en_us/article/homeless-uk-nick-hilton-356.

"Homeless and Runaway Youth." National Conference of State Legislatures, April 14, 2016. http://www.ncsl.org/research/human-services/homeless-and-runaway-youth.aspx.

"Homelessness in America." National Coalition for the Homeless. Retrieved March 16, 2017. http://nationalhomeless.org/about-homelessness/.

"How Many Homeless People Are There in America?" *Economist*, February 22, 2016. http://www.economist.com/blogs/democracyinamerica/2016/02/counting-street-sleepers.

HUD. "The 2016 Annual Homeless Assessment Report (AHAR) to Congress: PART 1: Point-in-Time Estimates of Homelessness." US Department of Housing and Urban Development, November 2016. https://www.hudexchange.info/resources/documents/2016-AHAR-Part-1.pdf.

Lohmann, Raychelle Cassada. "Homeless Teens." *Psychology Today*, January 9, 2011. https://www.psychologytoday.com/blog/teen-angst/201101/homeless-teens.

"Mobile Adolescent Health Services Program—Teen Van." Stanford Children's Health. Retrieved March 18, 2017. http://www.stanfordchildrens.org/en/service/teen-van.

"Mortgage Crisis Overview," Balance. Retrieved March 14, 2017. https://www.thebalance.com/mortgage-crisis-overview-315684.

"NCH Fact Sheet #13: Homeless Youth." National Coalition for the Homeless, August 2007. http://www.nationalhomeless.org/publications/facts/youth.pdf.

"NCH Fact Sheet #18: The McKinney-Vento Act." National Coalition for the Homeless, June 2006. http://www.nationalhomeless.org/publications/facts/McKinney.pdf.

"One Teen's Story: Homeless, Abused Teen Embraces New Life at Perennial House." Healthy Babies Project. Retrieved March 16, 2017. http://www.healthybabiesproject.org/stories-of-success/one-teens-story-homeless-pregnant-teen-embraces-new-life-at-perennial-house/

United Nations. "The Universal Declaration of Human Rights." December 10, 1948. http://www.un.org/en/universal-declaration-human-rights/.

US Department of Housing and Urban Development. "Title VIII: Fair Housing and Equal Opportunity." September 25, 2007. https://portal.hud.gov/hudportal/HUD?src=/program_offices/fair_housing_equal_opp/progdesc/title8.

Index

About the Author

Marcia Amidon Lüsted is the author of many books and magazine articles. articles for young readers. She has also worked as a teacher, a bookseller, and a magazine editor. She is a writer and editor for adults, as well as a musician and a permaculturist.

Photo Credits

Cover Federic J. Brown/AFP/Getty Images; pp. 5, 66–67, 68–69 © AP Images; pp. 8–9, 58 Spencer Platt/Getty Images; p. 10 Monkey Business Images/Stockbroker/Thinkstock; pp. 12–13 The Washington Post/Getty Images; pp. 16–17 Pierre Crom/Getty Images; p. 19 KatarzynaBialasiewicz/iStock/Thinkstock; p. 25 Nathan Ben /Corbis Historical/Getty Images; p. 28 Florilegius/SSPL /Getty Images; pp. 30–31 Alan Levenson/The LIFE Images Collection /Getty Images; pp. 34–35 Isa Foltin/German Select/Getty Images; pp. 38–39 Justin Sullivan/Getty Images; p. 41 stacey_newman /iStock/Thinkstock; pp. 44–45 Sabphoto/Shutterstock.com; pp. 48–49 AntonioGuillem/iStock/Thinkstock; p. 51 fhogue/iStock /Thinkstock; pp. 52–53 thefinalmiracle/iStock/Thinkstock; pp. 56–57 Grand Warszawa/Shutterstock.com; pp. 62–63 SpeedKingz /Shutterstock.com; pp. 72–73 NurPhoto/Getty Images; pp. 76–77 Silent47/iStock/Thinkstock; p. 79 Charlotte Observer/Tribune News Service/Getty Images; pp. 82–83 Bloomberg/Getty Images; p. 84 Rick Friedman/Corbis News/Getty Images; p. 86 © iStockphoto.com /dan_prat; pp. 88–89 Oppdowngalon/iStock/Thinkstock; pp. 90–91 Giles Clarke/Getty Images; cover and interior pages background © iStockphoto.com/Sergei Dubrovski.

Design and Layout: Nicole Russo-Duca; Editor and Photo Research: Heather Moore Niver